MODERN MYTHS

THE ART OF
RONALD PENNELL
IN GLASS AND BRONZE

On The Edge – A Realisation of Humanist Intention

MODERN MYTHS

THE ART OF
RONALD PENNELL

IN GLASS AND BRONZE

ANTIQUE COLLECTORS' CLUB

ISBN 1 85149 330 1

British Library Cataloguing-in-Publication Data
A catalogue record for this book is available from the British Library

Title page illustration: **Toe to Toe**, see page 53

Printed in England
by the Antique Collectors' Club Ltd., Woodbridge, Suffolk
on Consort Royal Satin paper
supplied by the Donside Paper Company, Aberdeen, Scotland

CONTENTS

ACKNOWLEDGEMENTS

The Artist wishes to thank:

The staff and students at the Academy of Arts, Architecture and Design in Prague for being exceptional role models in combining the standards of the classical with the avant garde.

At the University of Wolverhampton: Andrew Brewerton, Prof. Keith Cummings, Senior Research Fellow, Stuart Garfoot and members of his staff in the Glass Department for their constant help, advice and encouragement. Vanessa Cutler for her expertise with glass painting, unfailing optimism, and positive thinking. Tony Adams and Anthony Beckett for their practical skills and technical knowledge. Peter Olley and three remarkable members of staff from the School of Printmaking: Stewart Mason, James Abernethy and Andrew Roberts, also Dennis Farrell and Pamela Salter of the School of Ceramics.

A very special thanks to Jaqueline Cooley for her outstanding help and advice about Kiln Casting and without whom recent cast works would not have been possible.

At Wolverhampton Art Gallery thanks go to all staff involved in organising the exhibition, in particular to Pauline Thomas and Angela Spain. Also the Crafts Council and West Midlands Arts for their financial support.

The project would not have happened without Julia Ellis who, in addition to her role as curator, developed the exhibition concept with Martin Ellis, as well as the partnerships to make it happen. Similarly the realisation of this publication is due to the continuing and much valued support of Dan Klein and Alan Poole, my thanks go to them both. Also to Diana Steel at the Antique Collectors' Club and to all the contributors to the book who have valiantly placed my work in its context in the 1990s.

A thank you to all colleagues and friends who continue to support my work and in particular to Karin and James Webster and to Jiří Harcuba whose profound intelligence and wide cultural experience place him in a unique position as a portrait engraver without equal and a model of the best that one could wish for as a friend.

In the UK I should like to recognise the special contributions of Pauline Solven, Harry Cowdy, and Karlin Rushbrooke.

Cliff Guttridge is an outstanding photographer and friend who has documented my work for twenty-five years.

My wife Betty, a painter and print maker, who is the most important person in my life.

FOREWORD

by Julia Ellis
Curator of the Exhibition

Ronald Pennell is arguably the most celebrated engraver of glass working in Britain today, although this achievement represents only one aspect of his work. His œuvre spans a range of media, from medals to gemstones and glass, unique within British contemporary craft practice. Pennell brings an artistic vision, sharp wit, consummate skill and a highly idiosyncratic iconography to a tradition which has its roots in both courtly and popular work of the 17th and 18th centuries, and which continues to flourish within European culture.

In spite of this achievement, Ronald Pennell's work has received little formal, contextualised exposure in this country although his works have been acquired by many of our major public collections. On the world stage however he has been received with the greatest critical acclaim and continues to be awarded the most prestigious of international prizes. His particular affinity with the Czech Republic and the artistic traditions of Central Europe has led to special honours and an important relationship with that country, described at greater length later in this text.

A critical assessment of Ronald Pennell's work here is therefore timely, if not overdue. This book provides the first comprehensive survey of his art and its publication coincides with the launch of a major retrospective exhibition organised by Wolverhampton Art Gallery and funded by the Crafts Council and West Midlands Arts, and touring to major galleries within the UK and to the Museum of Decorative Arts in Prague. Ronald Pennell's work will be brought to the attention of a wider public than ever before.

This book and the exhibition also present the new cast glass forms for the first time, in the context of the engraved works, both recent and retrospective. They are important in several ways: not least in that, although his first cast glass pieces, they show the strength of his work in the round and, as described by Keith Cummings below, Pennell is probably the only artist in glass to combine casting with engraving techniques. This work has resulted from his on-going Visiting Professorship at the Glass Department within the School of Art and Design at the University of Wolverhampton.

The exhibition includes a number of loans from public collections, which are generally available to the public. However, reproduced on the following pages are many works now in private ownership which are, of necessity, less readily accessible, and in some cases untraceable. This publication therefore offers an opportunity to assemble a unique review of Pennell's output – recorded through Cliff Guttridge's photographs, which are themselves influential. The two-dimensional image offers us the opportunity to transcend a sense of object or material and to engage fully and freely with the art of Ronald Pennell, in its depiction of fallible humanity, just as he would wish.

THE ART OF RONALD PENNELL

by Dan Klein

Ronald Pennell discovered quite early on in life that the only way to combine all his enthusiasms and avoid compromise was to create a world of his own. This was not a form of escapism but an act of faith, belief in a lifestyle which would enable him to work exactly as he wished without interference from the restrictions of established convention. He lives peacefully with his wife Betty and their white Jack Russell, Bruno, in a cottage so near the River Wye in Herefordshire that the winding river landscape with its green fields and gently rising hills seems to come in through the window. On the hillside behind their cottage they have lovingly created a garden of which they are justly proud. Ronald's studio is a few steps away from the front door; it is tiny, tidy and ergonomically perfect. Rows of tools line the tongue and groove panelling; there are books and workspaces and there is computer equipment. One can imagine him spending hours and hours there happily absorbed in his work. Not far away is a typical English country village with its cast of squires and locals. Ronald and Betty understand them and like them.

Gem-engraving is a most unusual medium for an artist with a need to express himself, but for Ronald Pennell it is doing what comes naturally and one understands why. As soon as he could hold a pencil he began drawing people and he has never stopped. He says he was an extremely happy child. He was born in Birmingham and loves the coincidence of Betty having been born in the same nursing home. His father was a Royal Marine and his mother came from a family of printers. Recognising his talent, they sent him to the Moseley School of Art where youngsters between the ages of 12 and 17 spent three days a week doing art and two days a week on general subjects. Looking back on that early part of his education, Ronald feels that this curriculum resulted in a kind of cultural burn-out. One learnt incredible skills at an early age whilst losing the magic and joy of creation. The set tasks at school required technique, not imagination, so that style took over from meaning. This was a kind of art and craft design apprenticeship and it was a logical step, while working for the engraving instructor at Birmingham College of Art, School for Jewellery and Silversmithing, to take a course in Design taught by the distinguished silver designer Cyril Shiner (himself a pupil of another well-known British silversmith, Bernard Cuzner).

Despite this thoroughly British art and craft training Ronald Pennell is not a typically British craftsman or artist. Perhaps this is because his real artistic awakening was during his first visit abroad, to Germany. After his art school studies he had won a major scholarship to study gem-engraving with the Master Hermann Waldmann in Idar Oberstein, the heartland of the German precious gem industry. He had left Britain as an Englishman but returned after one and a half years a European and something of a stranger in his own land. Hearing the German language and absorbing German attitudes to culture in the art galleries there (which at the time were so much more part of normal life than they were in Birmingham) had a profound effect on him. To this day it may be true that Ronald feels it is more natural to speak about art in German than in English. For the first time he saw the work of Käthe Kollwitz, Edvard Munch, Wassily Kandinsky and Paul Klee, whose diaries, with their account of the Bauhaus, he had read in their original German version. At the same time as he was learning to master the use of the fixed wheel used in gem-engraving, he was introduced to the work of Wilhelm Lehmbruck and Ernst Barlach (a sculptor, ceramist and graphic designer) and perhaps through them re-discovered his own innate leaning towards a more sculptural idiom. Ronald feels he has always thought like a sculptor. He doesn't have to do a drawing to understand a form and sees things in three-dimensional terms. This formative period in his life as an artist has left its mark on the squat muscular figures that to this day are the hand-writing of his figurative art form.

On returning to England, Pennell was offered a lectureship at Birmingham College of Art where he met his wife Betty (who was appointed at the same time, after having graduated at the Royal College of Art where she had studied illustration, painting and print-making). Pennell loves teaching and early on in his career held a strongly-felt ambition to become a teacher, but his deeply ingrained suspicion of conventional structures made it impossible for him to accept the military hierarchy of the college. Now that he is older and does not need to feel so restricted by the socio-economic politics and pressures of academic life, he feels able to communicate more closely with young students at the University of Wolverhampton, where in 1998 he was appointed a Professor. Ronald had been appointed as a full-time lecturer at the age of 24 at the Birmingham College of Art, but both he and Betty decided their outlook on life was not compatible with college life. Instead they opted for poverty if not penury in the beautiful Wye Valley. They were both interested in classical music and literature and were unaffected by fashion and stylistic change, valuing artistic integrity above all.

If this all sounds desperately serious, one only has to know Ronald and Betty to realise what an enchanted and happy life they lead. Major Egmont Brodie-Williams typifies Ronald's mix of real concern for burning issues and amused tolerance of man at his most ridiculous. One of the central themes in Pennell's work is the way in which man the hunter destroys animal life without a thought for endangered species, whilst selfishly and thoughtlessly preserving his own to a degree which will cause over-population, famine and auto-destruction.

9

Often as one sits in Ronald's cottage the idyllic silence is interrupted by the not so distant pop of 12-bore guns aimed at pheasant. Not surprisingly, Ronald and Betty are vegetarians. For two years in the late 1970s Major Egmont Brodie-Williams, whose character was loosely based on a real person, was the central figure in the narrative created by Ronald Pennell. By means of exquisite gem-engraving Pennell followed his hero, accompanied by Monty the dog, on an odyssey through the South American jungle in pursuit of a rare and non-existent blue butterfly. The Major's immense and ridiculous acts of bravery in the face of crocodiles and other dangers are chronicled with tongue in cheek.

But before finding his niche as a gem-engraver on glass, Ronald Pennell spent the intervening years, between leaving Birmingham in 1964 and doing his first engravings on glass, working on gold and silver, carrying out numerous commissions before cutting a series of steel dies for original medals. As with everything, he was not content to stick to tradition and found that the most pleasurable way of creating medals was to cast them in bronze, whilst spending the bulk of his time developing the idea of using gem-engraving techniques on crystal. This technique had already been used on rock crystal for centuries, so its extension on to glass forms was logical and yet highly original, the more so because Ronald Pennell is a British artist and glyptic art is virtually unknown in this country. It is a tradition that has been developed principally in Northern Europe and during this century in the Czech Republic in particular. Ronald Pennell has been honoured with a professorship at the Prague Academy of Applied Arts, of which he is especially proud, and other parts of this catalogue bear testimony to his close links with the Czech Republic and the extent to which his art is appreciated outside this country.

From the start and in all areas of his artistic creation Ronald Pennell's aim is to transcend skill. For him skill in any art form that he practises or understands is essential and of seminal importance, and yet it should be so developed that it never draws attention to itself. He extends his skill by meeting new artistic challenges, the only ones that matter in his way of thinking. Ronald Pennell is lucky that his eyesight is so good that to this day he does not wear glasses. His initial public exposure as an engraver was a surprise invitation by the Crafts Council in 1974 to do a solo show. In 1979 two out of the three slides he submitted for inclusion in the Corning Museum's exhibition of contemporary glass 'New Glass: A Worldwide Survey' were accepted, which led eventually to an American trip and an invitation (which he refused) to design for Steuben Glass. Pennell was amused that a factory-made glass worth £2 that he had engraved should be chosen for a world-class show by the Corning Museum's panel of experts. The exhibition itself and the trip to the United States revealed a whole new world, the world of contemporary glass, so familiar today that one easily forgets how little known it was in Great Britain at the end of the 1970s. It was around this time that Pennell's direction as an artist became clearly defined.

But change has always been of the utmost importance in Pennell's artistic creation. He never allows himself, never wants to stay with any one idea for too long. In his prolific mind one thought leads the way to another more interesting one and this retrospective exhibition charts his artistic progression from medallic art to engraving on simple forms to working with glass-blowers who created more challenging shapes for him to use as his 'canvas', to a very recent discovery when he has found new release in using cast glass techniques to tell his story in a more sculptural idiom.

As a portraitist and figurative artist Pennell works from memory. He can draw a proper portrait but that is not what interests him. The memory is in a sense his mind's eye. On a vase done at the time of Prince William's birth he engraved Prince Charles completely from memory, thereby setting him into his own world and turning him into a typical Ronald Pennell figure, whilst still retaining his distinctive profile. His animals too are drawn from memory, and memory lapses, like the wrong positioning of a Rhinoceros' eye, add innocent charm and humour to his portrayals. In some ways it is an instinctive return to the artistic immediacy of his childhood, a way of trying to re-capture lost innocence. The people and animals Pennell draws represent human attributes rather like the gods of Greek mythology. The naked woman, always thought of by Pennell as a virgin, stands for innocence and purity, the crocodile represents innocent cruelty, the serpent usually synonymous with fear or horror also represents body warmth, the dog is man's best friend.

Whilst German Expressionists have had an obvious influence on Pennell, the influence of British art and many 20th century British artists is perhaps even stronger. His figural forms may often have a link with German artists and sculptors already referred to, but Pennell's lyricism is British. The first artist to have a real influence on him was William Blake and in tracing imagery which had an effect on him Pennell makes special reference to the two winged figures flying above a lake from Dante's Divine Comedy Series which had made such an impression upon him as a child. On first being exposed to the work of William Blake as a youngster he had found it quite simply amazing to see men with wings and thinks that probably the urge to add wings to humans has remained with him ever since. The fact that he had made a study of the early engravers had influenced Blake's drawing skills and somehow Pennell suspects this had struck a chord with him too. Also, for a young man living in Birmingham, the city's collection of Pre-Raphaelite paintings (where wings also abound) left its mark on an artistic talent in the making. Having thought about it Ronald Pennell comes up with Edward Burra and Stanley Spencer as his 'absolute personal favourites', but he also mentions Arthur Boyd, the early Sydney Nolan's and Howard Hodgkin. It is rare to find a contemporary glass artist talking as passionately about painting as Pennell does.

Interestingly enough, Pennell says that much as he loves colour he thinks in black and white, tone and form, not in colour. These are the words of somebody steeped in the less polychrome disciplines of engraving and sculpture. Although his work is busy with narrative, this is not seen by him as decoration. Figures in his work are like words on a page, and his love of poetry and literature are reflected in the logical syntax or positioning he chooses. He is an excellent story teller, a cross between Æsop in his fables and Edward Lear in his nonsense poems, a neo-classicist with a typically British sense of the ridiculous.

No other nation could have bred a Ronald Pennell, with his mix of non-conformity, civilised behaviour and irreverent sense of humour. His narrative, rather like that of Stanley Spencer, uses village life and the British landscape as its setting. Spencer interpreted the Bible in his paintings; Pennell uses the Herefordshire countryside, country life and local characters to chart a wide panorama of contemporary human attitudes in his work. His heart is in England, but his soul is rooted in the pan-European culture that so impressed him as a young man and has always continued to colour his thinking.

Ronald Pennell and Bruno, 1995

RONALD PENNELL AND JULIA ELLIS
IN CONVERSATION

J.E. You have worked in an unusually diverse range of media, from engraving metal, gems and glass vessels to recent cast glass forms. Can you explain the motivation to do this?

R.P. At Junior art school I happened to hear I could become an assistant to a teacher of engraving and the word itself captured my imagination. That random event led to working as an engraver for five years with a passionate interest in the subject. I began as a metal engraver and realised it was becoming an obsolete craft. As a result of being an engraver on silver and gold I became a designer of silver and a lecturer at a college, but in between time – the second random event – was a major scholarship which led me to Germany. I spent a year and a half in Germany learning gem-engraving, which is one of the oldest traditions of sculpture dating back to the early civilisations in the Middle East. But at that time I had no idea I would ever use the technique.

How was the period in Germany influential?

Firstly, I changed from being a classically trained engraver to becoming interested in contemporary art and design, the German expressionists, the artist Paul Klee, and European sculpture and painting, all to a much deeper level. Secondly, although gem-engraving had a wonderful tradition, artistically it had not progressed. It wasn't until seven years later that I realised it was capable of being relevant to the present time, then, for a period of ten years, while living here in Herefordshire, I engraved all kinds of gems but specialised in rock crystal engraving.

How important to you is living in the country?

Having taught at college for several years, in 1964 my wife and I both decided to end our teaching careers, move to the country and explore our artistic potential. Living in the country is of first importance. When I moved here I realised the value of the early childhood years of joy and happiness, and in my work began to try to recapture freshness and spontaneity of perception.

Would you describe yourself as a romantic artist?

Yes, in that my work is to do with states of innocence. But country life is not the Garden of Eden. For me this is real life and city life is the fantasy. For example I have seen sheep in the fields here for 35 years. Last year I witnessed a ewe on her back and as I approached to restore her to her feet, I realised that the animal, although alive, had had her eyes pecked out by crows. Country life is an ever changing kaleidoscope of sublime or brutal images. Experiences and memories lie dormant for years and then may appear in my work.

It's well known that, in your early career, you drew many people around rural Herefordshire who appear on the gems. It's extraordinary to me how majestic these – predominantly single – figures are, and yet your depiction

of them is, at the same time, within a hair's breadth of being caricature.

Gem engravings were collected by Kings and Emperors. They were always used to depict portraits of great people, notably the cameo portraits of Elizabeth I and her court. I thought it was an interesting idea to put the ordinary people back on to the gems because the earliest use of gem-engraving was both as a language, with the cylinder seals, but then, as with the Greek gems, to portray scenes of everyday life. So all I was doing really was to say that, well, you can take a perfectly normal person and put them on to a gem engraving.

This seems apparent in your medals as well.

But the medals again are traditionally used for commemorating significant events. In recent times there are many artists using medals as an art form. These medals should be seen as small sculptures, capable of combining the qualities of freshness, spontaneity and interesting ideas.

How much would you consider your choice of medium to be related to the meaning of the work?

In a way it's a subversive attitude to art. In contemporary life many artists are concerned with making important statements of great significance. Anything that doesn't fit within the obviously understood parameters of what constitutes art is often considered irrelevant, but I've always felt that nothing in the world is irrelevant if someone chooses to take an interest in it. Nothing in the world is obsolete while there is one human being willing to explore it.

How has your experience of gem-engraving influenced your work in glass?

The benefit of those years of discipline – engraving on to tiny surfaces using probably the most difficult engraving technique – meant that when I took to glass I found the technique comparatively easy. I could use it purely to express ideas, as I didn't have to think about the skill required. So therefore I had the freedom which transcends skill. I believe that you should be so sure of the idea that the skill is just a means of expression.

It seems extraordinary to me that, when you are engraving glass, you can't see what you are doing: because of the need to work with water you have water running over the vessel and obscuring the surface as you are working.

Yes but you are seeing it in the mind's eye all the time. In fact gem-engraving requires an even more delicate sense of touch as the stone is obscured by oil, so again this was an excellent training ground for glass.

In your free-blown engraved glass vessels, how are the narrative and formal elements reconciled?

Life is a story. Reality is a confusion of memory and images and the only difference between narrative and actuality is perception. I have kept an illustrated daily diary for nearly 30 years which acts as a trigger to memory. We are living with narrative the whole time. In terms of the formal reconciliation, all work – whether conceptual or realistic – is a small drama. The right sense of critical mass heightens the drama. The Japanese print-maker Hokusai was a master of critical mass and negative space. The blank areas should be as important as the image itself.

How do you set about achieving this reconciliation in your working practice?

A work of art should be like a footprint in the sand, incredibly fresh and direct. Many engravers make a drawing and copy the drawing on to glass. Inevitably that means something is lost in the translation because the artist is the slave to the pre-ordained image. When I work, I mark the critical mass on to the glass so that I know roughly where everything is going, but the images are engraved with direct cutting and without any reference to drawing at all. The focal point is the image in the mind and this is a very profound thing because there is a huge element of risk. My designs may look as if they have been designed and then applied to the glass but in fact they haven't been. It's a random event, and in your terms you may say it's very risky but in my terms it's just what I do.

The content of your work demonstrates a preoccupation with the accolades of society and the sense of a perceived pecking order. Would you say you believe in championing the underdog?

The works point out the ironies and paradoxes of life, and that things which are apparently humorous are actually deeply serious. If you decide to be an artist you are always and forever outside society. As one young army officer said to someone about me when he heard I was an artist – 'well it's hardly a profession is it' – so you are outside society.

Is your work politically driven, then?

In the sense of being Utopian and wanting a fair and just society, yes I am a political artist. I think that the small things, the quality of life, the way we behave to each other are the most important and only things of value that a society has.

Are you ever concerned or frustrated at your work not being fully understood, that people do not probe beyond the more humorous aspects to understand the philosophical intentions?

Different things appeal to different people. For instance, having worked in Germany, which is a sort of second cultural home, it has taken me a long time to realise that because generally there is a way of thinking which is literal, the humour in my work has often been misunderstood there because it is a very English humour. Conversely, working and being involved with the Czech Republic for a very long time, I found an immediate understanding and response from the Czechs because they understand the various levels of my work. At the first level it appears to be literal and sometimes humorous. But at the second level it is a black humour which is very serious indeed. Of course the Czechs perfectly understand this, and I think that is why I have a special relationship with that country. I cannot say how the British perceive what I am doing. I think in Britain probably the skill is admired, and maybe the humour is understood to a certain extent because it is a very British, situational humour.

Do you have any plans for the future?

Life is a constant road to nowhere and it's always interesting to see what happens next. I don't have targets. Life itself is a target.

The Relationship of Ronald Pennell to the History and Current State of Central European Thinking and Culture

by Sylva Petrova

'When I had attained that age at which the differences between good and bad begin to appear to the human understanding, it seemed most necessary to me to consider what group of men I should join, and with what matters I should occupy my life. Thinking much, and often on this matter, I came to the conclusion that the style of life having the least cares and violence, and most of well being, peace and happiness pleased me best. Thus I came to this decision: that I should first behold all earthly things under the Sun, and comparing one thing with another, choose a course of life providing the things necessary for leading a quiet life in the world.'

Johann Amos Comenius
The Labyrinth of the World and the Paradise of the Heart, 1631

The fates of the brightest star of European thinking in the 17th century, the Czech Johann Amos Comenius, and the English artist Ronald Pennell born three centuries later, are in many ways similar. Their life principles are founded upon the belief that the fleeting issues of this world, such as one's career, must be secondary to life itself. Despite, or perhaps because of the fact that the prevailing social situation differs from this principle they gained respect and recognition, and even many honours that they had not originally sought.

Pennell and Comenius share a criticism of general international vices, such as aggression. Each is concerned with human relationships and with the continual destruction of nature. Both recognise a need for the improvement of this world and possess an understanding that real peace and harmony can only be found within the human heart, whether one's own, those close to us, or through faith (represented by God in Comenius' and by nature and art in Pennell's case).

Pennell's stories, engraved or carved in glass, metal, wood, semi-precious stones and other materials, are not merely happy caricatures as some people mistakenly suppose. They are often allegories about people and animals through which he expresses his philosophy concerning contemporary problems: ecology, the destruction of wildlife and relationships between people.

Ronald Pennell has a sensitive personality, with nothing in common with leaders who voice their opinions over megaphones and manipulate people; he chooses a more subtle form of expression, mostly gentle and sometimes slightly ironic. His works may evoke laughter and a warm feeling in our hearts, but they also help us to question how, and why, we lead our lives.

It is natural that such an outlook on life points toward a need to communicate with other people and reveals an ability to teach others. Ronald Pennell is at present a Visiting Professor at the University of Wolverhampton. He has a reputation as a great teacher and is invited to many schools in Europe and the United States. Among other things, he is concerned with the structure of art

16

education and tries to find the best model for it. He is familiar with both the British and Czech education systems, being active in both countries and personally supporting art education in the Czech Republic through the British Association of Friends of the Prague Academy of Applied Arts (BAFPA-AA), which he founded in 1991 after the fall of communism in Czechoslovakia.[1]

The Association's aim has been to support Czech Art, and it is of great importance that in the present unfavourable economic climate it gives recognition and support to improving Anglo Czech relations by sponsoring one of Europe's leading art and design schools.[2]

Czech people think that the humour in Pennell's work is typically English, however in reality they understand it so well because Pennell's inspiration also contains many features in tune with continental thinking and in particular the Czech experience.

The Czech nation, whose long history includes only several decades of relative independence, has developed an in-built ability to turn difficult, sad, and hopeless situations into fun, and possesses a fine appreciation of allegory in both speech and behaviour, and the ability to create absurd situations. That is why, for example, the fictitious personality of 'the genius' Jara Da Cimrman (even the form of the name resembles Leonardo Da Vinci), whose actions inspired many plays of the Czech Theatre of the Absurd from the 1960s to the 1990s, and significantly influenced the intellectual atmosphere of those years in Czechoslovakia, appears to have so much in common with the figure of Major Egmont Brodie-Williams. This totally serious-looking gentleman, traveller, and hopeless loser experiences unbelievable adventures in which he is quite unaware that his self-importance and dignity are suffering great damage. These stories of the poor major were created by Ronald Pennell himself.

Thanks to sharing a similar sense of humour in their approach to life, several Czech artists and designers inspired Ronald Pennell to found the International Crocodile Club during his first visit to Prague in 1982. Why a Crocodile Club? The crocodile is a carefully thought-out symbol, an allegory of a predator who is, from a human standpoint, an innocent animal with no natural enemies. Its jaws are wide open to experience. Similarly artists should be innocent and wide open to new artistic, as well as personal experiences. One of its aims and achievements is to become an exclusive 'anti-club'. The most important rule is that no member of the club may wish to become a member; or admit to membership once invited to join! This idea came from Groucho Marx's famous remark that he would not want to belong to any club willing to have him as a member.

Like a citizen of Central Europe, Ronald Pennell shares a deep distrust of official authorities, using propaganda to spread their 'truths', and gestures to express 'great' feelings, which are usually a matter of show rather than real conviction; whose authors often attempt to manipulate and use this world for their own purposes. That is why Ronald Pennell always values 'modest art'.[3] For example the Czech painters, Vladimir Komarek, Josef Eapek and Jiri Sliva, or his wife, the painter Betty Pennell. These people take the path of silent concentration in a world of real values, that is close to his own thinking. He has a profound interest in modern art and a deep knowledge of contemporary art forms which can also be said of these artists.

Although the history of the re-discovery of glass engraving circa 1600 in Europe remains obscure, it is generally understood that it was first developed in the Germanic lands, especially Bohemia where the immigration of mainly

Italian engravers of semi-precious stones and rock crystal brought wheel engraving on glass for the first time to the court of Rudolph II. Wheel engraving also appeared for the first time in the works of the legendary Caspar Lehmann who made the transition from rock crystal to glass.

The history of English engraved glass dates back to the period before the beginning of the 16th century. Although in the 19th and 20th centuries there has been a rich production of outstanding works to form a sound basis for contemporary work, the present status of engraved glass in England and Europe is problematic. The production of original engraved glass has outstanding representatives in Jiři Harcuba and Ronald Pennell, as well as a few other artists. The further development and popularity of engraving suffers from the fact that most engravers focus on technical perfection, which in some cases is remarkable, but they overlook the real purpose and meaning of their work, for the present time. What they are doing mostly refers back to the 19th century. Naturally such perfect craftsmanship attracts its followers, but they are usually people outside artistic circles, and therefore have little influence.

In contrast, Jiři Harcuba and Ronald Pennell are both sculptors with a remarkable ability to express themselves through drawing. They have managed to make their works both personal and topical, while bringing to engraving new visual perceptions. This is why they are both acknowledged as the leading personalities in their field.

Pennell's abilities are, from an artistic viewpoint, very universal. Since on his path towards working with glass he has used many materials and techniques, because of this wide experience he has become liberated from technical problems in engraving. He uses engraving spindles with diamond wheels, and his cuts are precise and made without any additional forms of alteration such as matting or polishing. This working method requires a clear concept, since all stages of the work are final and cannot be corrected. It is a simple but demanding approach toward glass engraving, closer to Lehmann's technique, or that of the Egyptians, Greeks or Romans rather than the Czech, Swedish or German works of the last two centuries.

Ronald Pennell is an artist whose work is an example of a unique mixture of English and European cultures, in which tradition is combined with personality, and in which art lives in symbiosis with humanity and nature. The same principles also serve as a base for friendship between Ronald Pennell and the Czech artists Jiri Harcuba, Rene and Miluse Roubicek, and others. Although Pennell says that he has learned many things in Bohemia, he has, through his own life and work, certainly given us even more.

Notes

1) During the first years, Ronald Pennell became the chairman with a secretary. Honorary members included: Prof. Keith Cummings, Prof. Jiři Harcuba, Eva Jiricna RDI, Dr. Mark Jones, Prof. Dan Klein, and other personalities of European art and culture. Almost 70 members of this association have annually awarded £1000 prize money to the winners of competitions at the Academy of Art, Architecture and Design Prague. (VSUP) The annual competitions have themes decided upon by all of the Academy's departments and studios. They involve an inter-disciplinary approach to encourage young artists and designers. This applies to their professional, social, and artistic development, since the students judge the results too.

Pennell is a Professor of the Academy, a member of its Senate, and thus, as a foreign consultant, a significant contributor to its new orientation and conception.

2) In 1993 Ronald Pennell was awarded a professorial fellowship and Gold Medal for his work and contribution to the development of the Academy as well as Czech-British cultural links. At the International Symposium of Engraved Glass held in Kamenicky Senov in 1996, the Academy of Art, Architecture and Design in Prague awarded him the Highest Honour for the most outstanding collaborative work.

3) The term that was used by the Czech painter and art theoretician Josef Eapek in the 1920s and 1930s for the artistic works inspired by folk art, as well as by the naive art of old and so-called 'primitive' cultures.

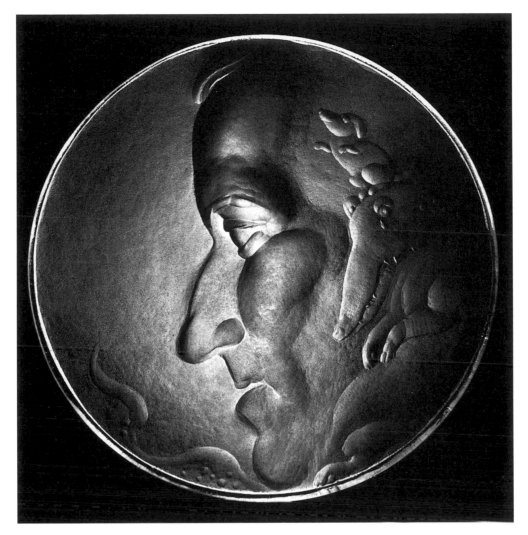

Portrait of Ronald Pennell on engraved crystal by Jiří Harcuba, 1982.

RONALD PENNELL
A PERSONAL TRIBUTE

by Jiří Harcuba

After an early career as a lecturer and metal engraver and many years working as a gem and rock crystal engraver, Ronald Pennell began to engrave glass in 1977 and in 1979 was selected for the most significant glass exhibition of the century NEW GLASS '79 at the Corning Museum of Glass, USA. He rapidly became an internationally recognised glass engraver.

Since then, he has created a great number of engravings which are an important contribution to contemporary glass art. His work is original in technique and also represents a new philosophical point of view.

Pennell is an excellent artist: with fascination we can observe his sense of humour which hides a deep wisdom and understanding of life. Drawings are his language, he draws every day and at every opportunity. His letters, which are always illustrated, express his ideas much better than words. From this daily activity he can take any image or idea for his engravings. With a few lines he will decide upon the critical masses in relation to a vessel and then, without reference to any drawings, engrave the glass with firm, precise cuts, using the minimum number of diamond wheels. He never 'improves' his work by erasing mistakes or polishing as most engravers do, he has transferred his mastery as a gem engraver to glass.

In 1982 he was the first British glass artist to be invited to Czechoslovakia for the International Glass Symposium at Novy Bor. After a few weeks studying the Czech language he was able to communicate with a few words and many humorous drawings. Everyone, but especially the professional engravers, wanted to watch him working with his personally designed engraving machine.

Pennell's world is full of irony and paradox. Those who understand the fact that humour can be very serious will see that his conversation and works have a deeper meaning; I can feel the same enlightenment with him as one can find with *Till Eulenspiegel*, *Don Quixote*, or *Josef Schweik*. In Czechoslovakia he has a much bigger audience than in Germany, where he studied. He could, like Mozart, say 'the Czechs understand me'.

Behind his smile there is compassion for man and nature, one of his engravings, 'Topiarist', shows a man cutting his own figure out of a hedge, symbolising *Homo sapiens* commemorating himself through his work. Pennell often portrays people in their daily lives, sometimes in strange situations but always with love. His figures are anti-heroes, similar to those in the novels of Karel Capek, so dear to the hearts of the Czech people; his compositions are spontaneous, with a strong characterisation, full of an understanding of ordinary men.

His most successful character was Major Egmont Brodie-Williams, engraved between 1977 and 1979. This anti-hero, while butterfly-hunting, is usually being chased by all kinds of wild animals; unaware of any danger, he is always protected by his faithful terrier Monty. After a final successful exhibition in London, Pennell never engraved another Brodie-Williams glass, it was time to move on.

Another engraving, 'Crocodile Carrier', shows a man carrying a crocodile 'looking for a place where it could live', a humorous story to make us think about serious problems. Crocodiles represent 'innocent cruelty' in contrast to the premeditated human kind. Pennell's themes are often founded upon a chase. The world seen as a relentless hunting ground, mankind in a never ending race towards oblivion, creatures and men running after each other, and for the present time escaping their fate.

Ronald Pennell is not only an excellent artist, but a fine teacher. He has taught mainly in England, Europe and the USA, sharing his ideas, wisdom and humour with many students who are his good friends.

Ronald Pennell, Artist in Glass

by Keith Cummings

This exhibition celebrates a career that to date encompasses four decades of achievement. The Glass area at the University of Wolverhampton School of Art and Design can trace its history back over 150 years, and the relationship with Ronald Pennell, although less than two years old, has been profound.

We approached Professor Pennell in 1997, upon hearing of his planned Retrospective Exhibition at Wolverhampton Art Gallery, to ask him if he would accept the title of Visiting Professor of Glass Studies. A two-fold collaboration was proposed: Pennell would be given access to the facilities and expertise of the staff to help him to develop and realise new types of work for his exhibition, while the School would benefit from the presence of an internationally respected glass artist.

Ronald Pennell's response to this challenge may be seen within the exhibition. In addition to the work for which he is renowned, characters from his personal world have made a seemingly effortless transition from two to three dimensions, at the same time undergoing a change of scale.

His new cast figures have an ease and sophistication that belie the difficulties of such an undertaking. Pennell's use of an engraving lathe to sharpen and define the cast surface is a skill available to few, if any, kiln casters. This diamond wheel engraving technique adds an important extra dimension to the sculptures. This is all the more remarkable when the difference between engraving (which creates an illusion through concavities in the glass surface) and full three-dimensional modelling (which is additive) is taken into account.

I have always admired intaglio engraving. Like etching, the artist works with a reversed image. Working on a static surface with a hand-held marker is one thing, it is quite another to manipulate a three-dimensional object against a fixed engraving wheel to carve its surface.

Because of the nature of the process, intaglio engraving impresses with its sheer difficulty; many engravers make a virtue of this demanding skill whilst few manage to move beyond it to achieve a mastery of technique that places engraving firmly within an artist's vocabulary. Ronald Pennell and the Czech sculptor and portrait engraver Jiri Harcuba belong to the select few who have done so.

In painterly terms I am reminded of the great English artist Ivon Hitchens, of whom the artist Patrick Heron commented, 'in his work paint becomes tree, and tree becomes paint'. This could be applied to the freshness and surety of Pennell's style. A series of lines and hollows carved into the glass surface forms a highly personal vocabulary. The character of the resulting images cannot be separated from the technique in the creative synthesis that brings them to life. As it is essentially a subtractive process there is no room for error; like Oriental brush painting the hand movement that creates the mark must be second nature.

The production of a body of new work, different in technique and scale to most of his œuvre, is only one aspect of Pennell's collaboration with the University of Wolverhampton. The impact of his frequent presence within the studios at the School of Art and Design has been significant. The result has

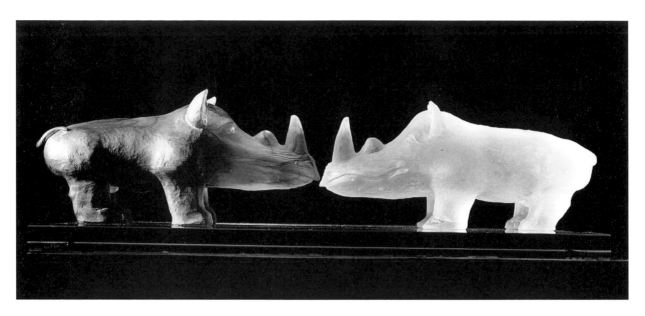

Twin Horns
Cast and carved glass on cut base, 50 x 23 x 15cm, 1999.

been a successful working relationship with the staff and a benign influence on the undergraduate and post-graduate students. His example of high quality practice has a subtle way of raising standards and morale that is difficult to categorise. In addition Professor Pennell has given lectures about major international contemporary artists and demonstrated new techniques that have added to the knowledge and atmosphere of the School as a whole.

For the University, the appointment of Ronald Pennell as a Visiting Professor has established a model of practice for the future.

THE MEDALLIC ART
OF RONALD PENNELL

by Mark Jones

Engraving has traditionally been fundamental to the medallic tradition. Engraved gems and Greek coins, with their lively yet stylised representations of animals, beautifully composed within the space that they inhabit, have been an endless source of inspiration for medallists through the ages.

Ronald Pennell himself, of course, an outstandingly accomplished engraver, astonishingly quick and fluid in his creation of forms in metal as well as in glass, has contributed greatly to the new wave of medallic work in late 20th century Britain.

His work as a medallic artist began with a series of children's rhyming medals with his own verses in the early 1970s, followed in 1976 by the Hereford Cathedral medal. This shows King Ethelbert, losing his head and so becoming a Saint and Martyr, in a composition that works beautifully with and against the rim of the medal.

Another medal of the period, a 'Good Growers' gardening medal (above, 1976), shows a man proudly holding a giant marrow. Whorling strands of marrow flesh make a wonderfully decorative, appropriate and mildly subversive reverse.

Landscape (1980) and Hedgehog by Moonlight (1980) were, like Pennell's previous medals, struck from steel and dies hand-engraved by the artist. His 'A Tree for Me', created in 1984 for the British Art Medal Society, achieves much higher relief, cast from a master the obverse of which was cast from an engraved glass lens, while the reverse was carved directly in silver.

Ronald Pennell's description of the medal is telling, not only about it but also about his other work. 'A tree for me shows a man wheeling away the last ancient tree in a wheelbarrow, perhaps for preservation in a museum! The serpent, with all it represents in mythology and Christianity, observes all. On the reverse three dead trees in a barren landscape. I am an optimist but everyone alive today must think from time to time – where, when and how will it all end?'

Pennell's more recent work 'A Bird in the hand is well worth two in the bush – but will they survive?' (1992), 'Two birds: Medallic Stele I' (1993) and 'Freeing the Birds' (1993) all convey this same mixture of gaiety and optimism combined with keen foreboding. Even the topiarist of 'Hedged In' (1993), happily engaged in the most innocent of pursuits, is imprisoned by his own work.

Life-enhancing and haunting, Ronald Pennell's medals are populated by a cast of characters new to the medallic tradition: apparently ordinary people caught up in extraordinary situations. Curiously combining gaiety and menace, they live on in the imagination, yielding up their meaning through time.

Two Birds
Medallic Stele 1
Cast bronze, 80mm high, 1993.

Medallic Stele 2
Cast bronze medal,
80 x 15mm, 1993.

Freeing the Birds
Cast bronze, 70mm diameter, 1993.

Oxford Medal
Cast bronze medal,
18mm diameter, 1992.

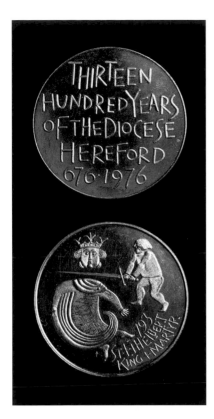

The Last Tree or A Tree for Me
Cast bronze medal, 1995.

A Bird in The Hand
*Cast bronze medal,
95mm diameter, 1992.*

**The Hereford Cathedral
Medal**
*Die cast silver medal,
50mm diameter, 1976.*

St Ethelbert King and Martyr

**Open Wide (International
Crocodile Club)**
*Cast bronze medal,
95mm diameter, 1992.*

Man's Best Friend
*Cast bronze medal,
55mm diameter, 1992.*

Hedged In
Cast bronze medal, 70mm diameter, 1993.

Windfall
*Cast bronze medallic relief
100mm diameter.*

The first couple having their
attention drawn towards the
windfall at their feet.

CATALOGUE NOTES

Works are in the possession of the artist unless otherwise stated.

All photography by Cliff Guttridge unless otherwise specified.

Until 1979 Ronald Pennell's glass engraving was executed on factory-made forms produced by: Crystallex Co., Strombergshyttan, Orrefors, Dartington Glass, Stuart Crystal, Rosenthal, and more recently Moser AG.

Mike Hoskins and staff of G. & B. Gardner & Newton Ltd (glass bending) are current collaborators on an architectural glass project.

Subsequently, blown glass vessels have been executed by the following artists in glass: Deborah Fladgate, Karlin Rushbrooke, Neil Wilkin and Simon Eccles.

Carl Nordbruch has made the most recent forms and is currently working with the artist.

For bronze casting, Tony Limb and Philip Hinks of Lunt's Castings for their advice and expertise.

Kazuyuki Okamato photographed 'On the Edge – A Realisation of Humanist Intention', which is reproduced with the kind permission of the Hokkaido Museum of Modern Art.

Technical Information

Gem engraving
Rock crystal is a natural quartz, a semi-precious stone exactly the same as Amethyst but without the colour. Its hardness is much greater than glass, H7 on the scale at which Diamond is H10. The Pennell Crystals are intaglio engraved in reverse, resulting in the image being magnified through the lens, making a greater demand than usual on the quality of the engraving.

Medals
The early medals were hand engraved on pairs of steel dies in the actual size (50mm) to make obverse and reverse designs, which were then struck on a Coinage Press at the City of Birmingham Polytechnic, which is now The University of Central England.

Cast glass Figures, Bronzes and Medallic Reliefs
These have all been modelled in clay, then a rubber mould was made, from which a wax was taken before the final investment moulds were made for casting – with the exception of The Last Tree which was cast from an impression taken from an engraved crystal.

THE CATALOGUE

EXHIBITION TOUR DATES

18 September – 13 November 1999   Wolverhampton Art Gallery

27 November – 24 December 1999   Phillips Auctioneers,
London

12 January – 12 March 2000   National Glass Centre,
Sunderland

25 March – 30 April 2000   National Museums of
Scotland, Edinburgh

13 May – 2 July 2000   Castle Museum and Art
Gallery, Nottingham

2001 – dates to be confirmed   Museum of Decorative Arts,
Prague

Apple – Circumstances Alter Cases
Bronze relief, cast and hand-finished, 30cm square, 1999.

The Flood
Bronze relief, cast and hand-finished, 30cm square, 1999.

Tiger Forest
Bronze relief, cast and hand-finished, 30cm square, 1999.

My Heart is like an Apple Tree
Cast bronze, hand-finished, 10cm diameter, 1999.

Medallic disc

Ritual Walk – The Golden Stick
Cast bronze, hand-finished, 10cm diameter, 1999.

Medallic disc

Tiger Trick
Cast bronze, hand-finished, 10cm diameter, 1999.

Medallic disc

Tiger Tail
Cast bronze, hand-finished, 10cm diameter, 1999.

Medallic disc

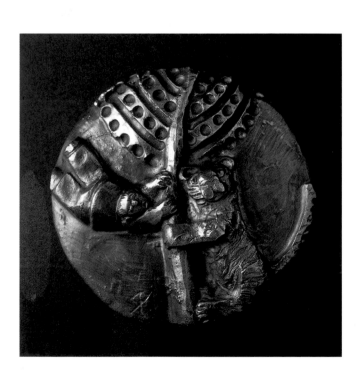

Tiger Tree
Cast bronze, hand-finished, 10cm diameter, 1999.

Medallic disc

Mask

Silver, chased, 20 x 15cm, London Hallmark RP circa 1961.

Made for an International Design Competition sponsored by the Gesellschaft fur Goldschmiedekunst, Hamburg.

As a young lecturer at the Birmingham College of Art, School of Jewellery and Silversmithing between the years 1959-64 Ronald Pennell exhibited his work in Germany. He also successfully competed in design competitions before leaving teaching to establish his own studio.

Market Day, Hereford
Rock crystal, reverse wheel engraved, 65 x 55mm, 1968.

Nightwatchman, a forgotten past
Rock crystal, reverse wheel engraved,
65 x 55mm, 1968.

Proud Scot
Rock crystal, reverse wheel engraved,
65 x 55mm, 1970.

Klondike Bill
Rock crystal, reverse wheel engraved,
65 x 55mm, 1972.

Major Egmont Brodie-Williams and the Butterfly
Rock crystal, reverse wheel engraved, 30 x 20mm, 1974.

Major Egmont Brodie-Williams Fishing
Rock crystal, reverse wheel engraved, 30 x 20mm, 1973.

Major Egmont Brodie-Williams and The Tiger
Rock crystal, reverse wheel engraved, 65 x 55mm, 1972.

Man with *The Times*
Rock crystal, reverse wheel engraved, 20 x 30mm, 1974.

Professor Ronald Pennell with his Assistant Jaqueline Cooley at the University of Wolverhampton.

Ronald Pennell in his Studio.

Top Dog
Wood, carved and painted, 64 x 34 x 18cm, 1990.

This was the first of a series of wood carvings. It was made to celebrate a fearless and loyal Jack Russell terrier – featured in many engravings.

Tree for a Garden Urn
Bowl, green over-cased glass, wheel engraved. Ht 16cm, 1982.
Private Collection

Into Africa
The Grand Fallacy
Bowl, rose-tint over-cased glass wheel engraved, 16 x 19cm, 1996.

A man holding a small rhinoceros while thinking of its aphrodisiac horn, is reprimanded by a modern Eve for what he has done to the Garden of Eden.

Natural Selection

Bowl, lime tinted glass, wheel engraved, 20.5 x 16.5cm, 1996.

All creatures are used as a means to human ends; wild ones are becoming extinct while other animals and birds rarely practise natural selection. Breeding is usually the result of unnatural selection culminating in the success of cloning.

Celtic Carnival

Bowl, amber over-cased glass, wheel engraved, 20.5 x 16.5cm, 1996.
Koganezaki Glass Museum, Japan

The artist is watching a carnival dragon with two Welshmen inside it.
Behind him there is an Anglo-Saxon bird man with the artist's dog,
Bruno. A latterday 'King Ethelbert' loses his head in response to a local
legend, while a virgin stands on the dragon's tail.

Strange Voyage
Bowl, sage over-cased graal glass, wheel engraved, 17.5 x 13cm, 1997.

Pulling Together
Bowl, green and brown over-cased, wheel engraved intaglio graal, 25 x 15cm, 1997.

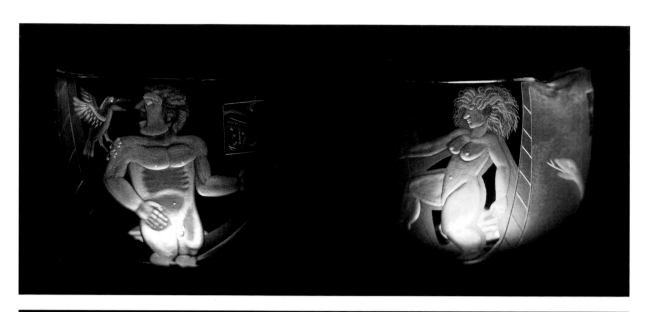

Window into Past and Future Time
Bowl, sage over-cased glass, wheel engraved, 18.5 x 22cm, 1998.

Through a window on the vessel the artist observes the human condition. Youthful hopes ambitions and ideals may be leading towards loneliness and old age. The Crow is a metaphor for the darker side of life. As country folk used to say when a move was contemplated; "The Crows are just as black over there..."

There's a Catch in This
Vessel, brown over-cased glass, 30cm, 1998-9.

Two of a Kind

Glass, cast and carved on cut base,   24 x 30.5 x 20cm,   1999.

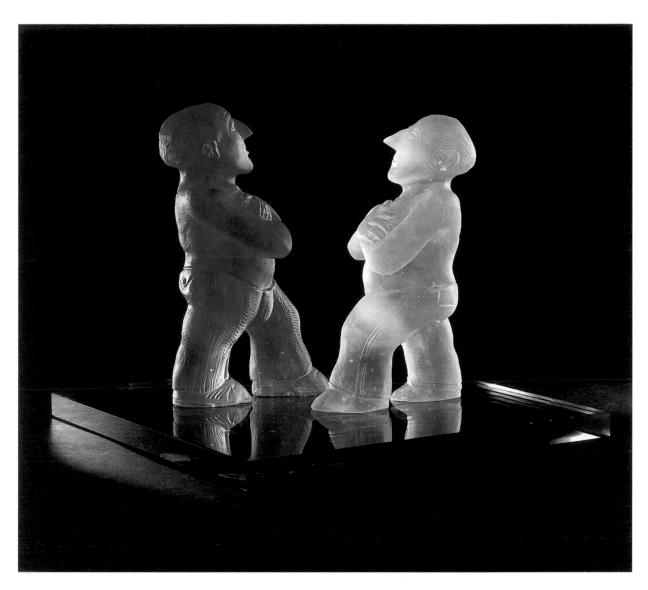

Toe to Toe
Glass, cast and carved on cut base, 25 x 30 x 30cm, 1999.

Jubilee Flu

Tumbler, clear glass, wheel engraved, 8 x 8cm, 1977.

The Jubilee glasses were among the first engraved glasses by Ronald Pennell. They were created to celebrate the Queen's Jubilee Year of 1977.

Pennell lies in bed with influenza on Jubilee Day while his wife and Monty bring him medicine.

Jubilee Dream

Tumbler, clear glass, wheel engraved, 8 x 8cm, 1977.

The worst is over and he dreams of peace and happiness as clouds and a bird pass by.

Jubilee Beans

Tumbler, clear glass, wheel engraved, 8 x 8cm, 1977.

Mr Ernest Pragnell stands by his runner beans which fly the flag in honour of the day. An abundant crop will not result, as a rabbit is busy destroying his hopes.

Jubilee Flock

Tumbler, clear glass, wheel engraved, 8 x 8cm, 1977.
Private Collection

Dr Crooke, with a crook in hand, walks his Jack Russell terrier Percy ahead of the
Jubilee Flock.

Married Bliss

Bowl, clear glass, wheel engraved. Ht 6cm, 1977.

Victorian Gothic beds and matching cot are the setting for this family. Under each bed is a night pot with a pet dog by the man, and a cat by his wife.

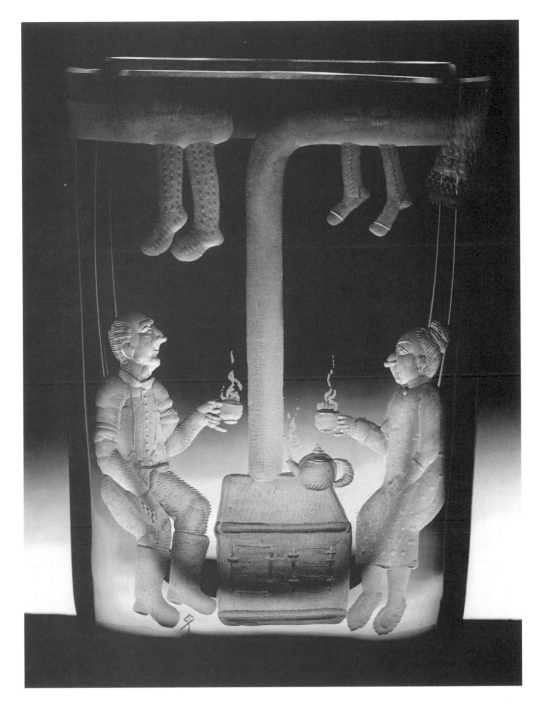

Tea Time
Vase, clear glass, wheel engraved. Ht 15cm, 1978.
Portsmouth City Museum and Art Gallery

This is a response to the Japanese tea ceremony. It is a couple taking morning tea by the Aga in a Herefordshire cottage, the knickers and socks hanging around the stovepipe are a far cry from the Japanese kimono but the man's extended little finger indicates a wish for gentility.

Oarsman with Ducks

Vase, clear glass, wheel engraved. Ht. 15cm, 1978.
Crafts Council Collection

A man stands like a warrior, his oar clutched as a spear symbolising the ritualised combat of sport, while a formation of ducks mocks this perfect specimen of man at his attempt to take to the water.

Major Egmont Brodie-Williams and the Warthogs
Goblet (detail), clear glass, wheel engraved. Ht 15cm, 1977.

Major Egmont Brodie-Williams and the Turtles
Goblet detail, clear glass, wheel engraved. Ht., 15cm. 1977.

The Major has fallen among fertile turtles…
one of a set of six goblets (1mm thick) called 'Major Egmont Brodie-Williams in Africa'
Engraved on very fragile glass, this was the first set of goblets engraved by the artist.

Major Egmont Brodie-Williams and the Wild Boars
Standing Bowl. W 10cm, 1979.
Private Collection

Major Egmont Brodie-Williams in Africa
Tumblers, clear glass, wheel engraved, 9cm, 1979.
Private Collection

Major Egmont Brodie-Williams and the Koala Bears
Vase, clear glass, wheel engraved. Ht 8cm, 1979.
Private Collection

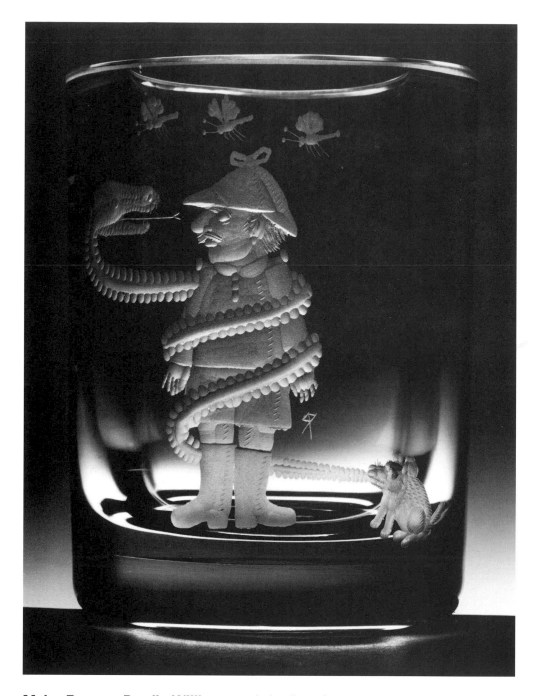

Major Egmont Brodie-Williams and the Boa-Constrictor
Straight sided vase, blue tinted glass, wheel engraved. Ht 10cm, 1979.
Private Collection

The intrepid Major seems to have a problem. His dog, while trying to release him from the boa-constrictor's coils is, of course, pulling the wrong way…
The Major was a mixture of fact and fiction. Firstly engraved on rock crystal, he became a hero on Pennell glass with adventures taking place from 1977 to 1979. Too popular for the artist's liking, it became necessary to abandon him and his dog while they were on a butterfly hunt in the Amazonian jungle in search of the rare 'Brodie-Williams Blue' (named after one of the Major's ancestors).

Butterflies and Pigs

Square vessel, clear glass, wheel engraved. Ht 10cm, 1979.
Private Collection

A young farmer feeds a smug sow with nuts in his free time, a sublime form of the day to day toil of farming. Man and beast exist in complete harmony with the butterflies symbolising the peace which reigns between them.

Congratulations
Straight sided vase, blue tinted glass, wheel engraved. Ht 12cm, 1979
Private Collection

This happy couple have twins. While he congratulates her, their twin cats look on.

Topiarist, Homo Sapiens
Bowl, clear glass, wheel engraved. Ht 8.5cm, 1979.
Private Collection

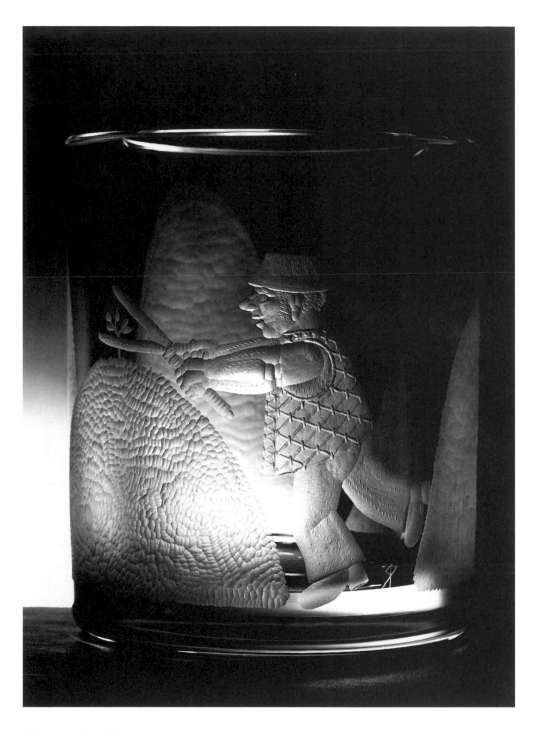

The Last Leaf
Straight sided vase, blue tinted glass, wheel engraved. Ht 15cm, 1979.
Private Collection

Scrumping
Goblet (detail), clear glass (1mm thick), wheel engraved. Ht 17cm, 1980.

Spring Fever
Tall goblet, clear glass (1mm thick), wheel engraved. Ht 13.5cm, 1980.
Private Collection

Country life. On a glass as fragile as the English countryside a Herefordshire local thinks of the past while his pigs jump for joy in the meadow.

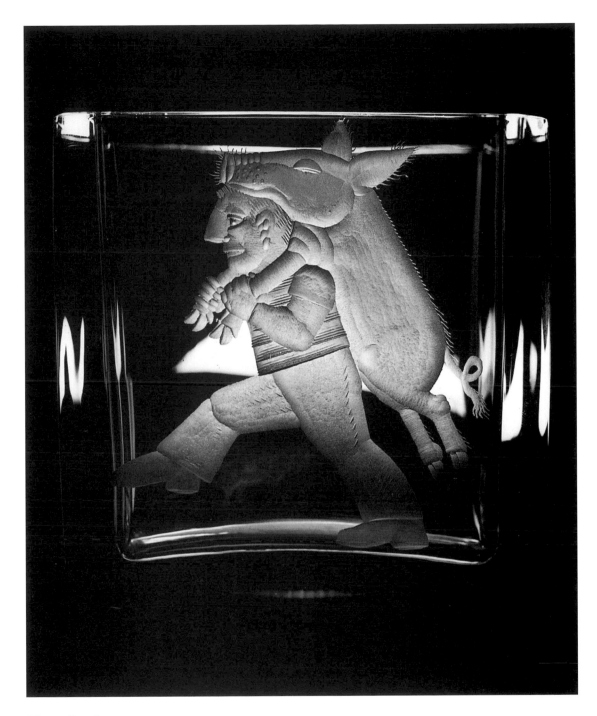

Piggy Back
Square vessel, clear glass, wheel engraved, 12.5 x 6cm, 1980.

The artist once rescued a pig with its leg broken and caught in a wire fence. In this idealised version the poor animal is being carried away to be helped while a little pig looks on and butterflies flutter by.

Jaws II
Vase, clear glass, wheel engraved. Ht 20cm, 1980.
Private Collection

Talking to the Birds

Decanter, clear glass, wheel engraved, 24 x 13 x 6cm, 1981.

Communing with nature while his dog stands by, a latterday St Francis of
Assisi seems to be unaware that the ornamentation on this decanter is
providing an unusual habitat for the birds. One way of showing that 'kitsch for
the rich', e.g. conventionally 'pointless' decoration, can be made relevant.

Crocodile Carrier
Straight sided container, blue tinted glass, wheel engraved. Ht 16.5cm, 1981.

In the Year of the Drought he carries a crocodile to a fresh pool.

I Serve

Bowl, royal pink over-cased glass, wheel engraved. Ht 15cm, 1982.

HRH Prince Charles, having returned from a Trooping the Colour, wheels his son and heir in a baby carriage decorated with the Prince of Wales crest with his motto *Ich Dien* on the side. Prince William waves the Union flag while three of the Queen's corgis stay in the background.

Over the Hills and Far Away

Bowl, blue tinted glass, wheel engraved, 14 x 11.5cm, 1984.

A man is seeking his ideal woman who is over the hills and far away, a metaphor for the unattainable. She is standing by a memorial urn, with the monogram RP. She is holding a falcon.

The Fisherman's Daughter
Bowl, blue tinted glass, wheel engraved. Ht 15cm, 1984.
Crafts Council Collection

The fisherman's daughter is caressing a Narwhal while her father clings desperately to its horn.
A small dog, unseen in this picture, joins in the swim.

There is a Willow

Bowl, blue tinted glass, wheel engraved. Ht 15cm, 1984.
Private Collection

There is a willow on the banks of the River Wye, but not
for much longer. This ancient tree may become as
legendary as the Harpy in its branches.

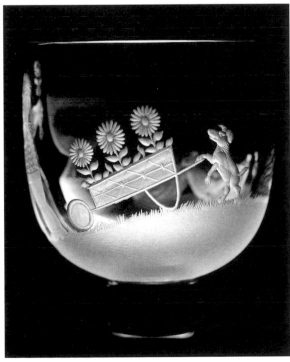

Flower for a Garden Urn

Bowl, blue over-cased glass, wheel engraved. Ht 14cm, 1984.

Inspired by John Keats' poem *Ode to a Grecian Urn*. The gardener offers a flower to the urn, helped by his terrier, while a friend takes a well-earned rest.

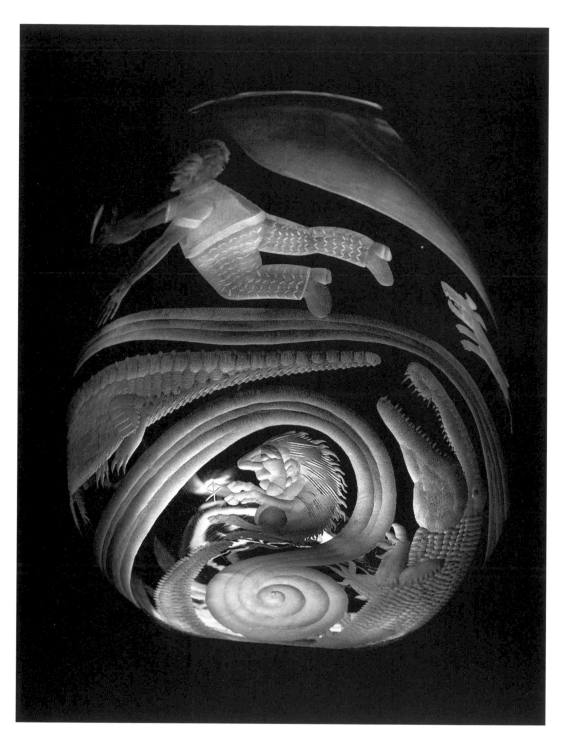

Walking The Earth – Bird Catcher
Bowl, green tinted glass. Ht 20cm, 1984.
Private Collection

Herefordshire Hydra
Bowl, green tinted over- cased glass, wheel engraved, 13 x 17cm, 1988.
Private Collection

An improbable event. Two Herefordians tangle with descendants of the Great Worm of Mordiford, based upon a local legend.

Crocodile Race

Bowl, amber glass, wheel engraved, 14 x 21cm, 1991.

Ronald Pennell's crocodiles are an idea or symbol, not intended to be a copy of the real thing. In Crocodile Race they are being held or followed by men in a race towards extinction.

Crocodile Catch
Bowl, topaz tinted glass, wheel engraved, 16 x 11cm, 1991.

The artist is about to hold fast to his creation, a crocodile!

Big Fish Eat little Fish

Bowl, lime tinted over-cased glass, 16 x 21cm, 1992.

There are many kinds of predator. The artist holds a large fish which is trying to eat a small one, quite unaware that both are in danger from the crocodile's gaping jaws. Monty his Jack Russell terrier rushes to the rescue.

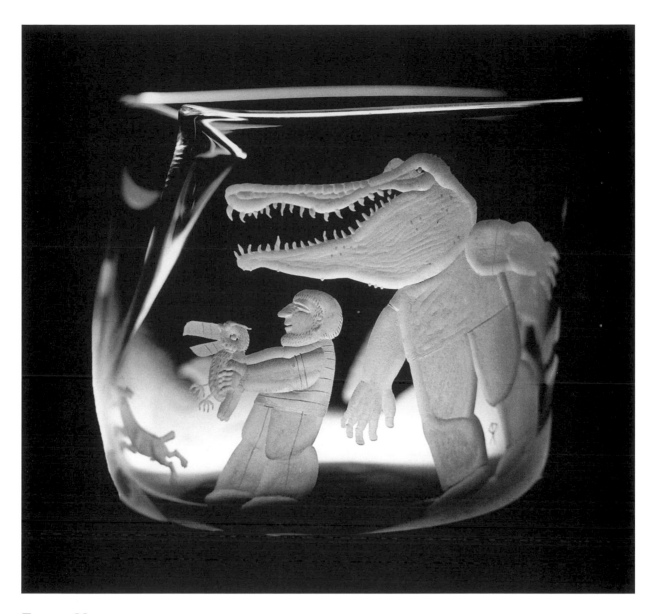

Toucan Moon

Bowl, clear glass, wheel engraved, 17 x 23 x 21cm, 1992.
Notojima Glass Museum

An unlikely event. While returning a toucan to the safety of its island, the artist sees a friend pointing to the moon. They are both unaware of the metamorphosis of crocodile-man and its significance.

Falling Leaves

Bowl, clear glass, wheel engraved, 14 x 12cm, 1993.

Time has no meaning to animals and birds, their lives are like the falling leaves, everything in its season.

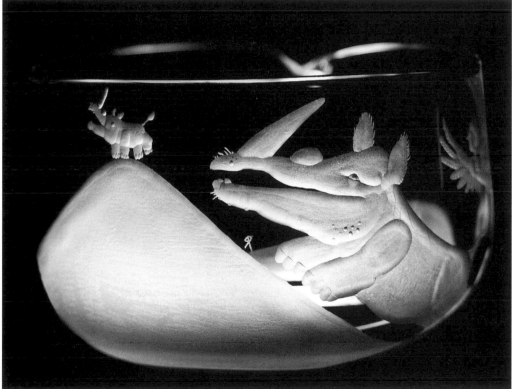

Unique Horn

Bowl, rose tinted glass, wheel engraved, 13 x 20cm, 1993.

A rhinoceros is charging towards a mythical future, finally it is seen as a small creature at the top of a hill. Nearby a harpy is in flight from its mythical past. Sadly it is possible that the rhinoceros with its 'unique horn' will join the unicorn and the harpy and become a chimera of the future.

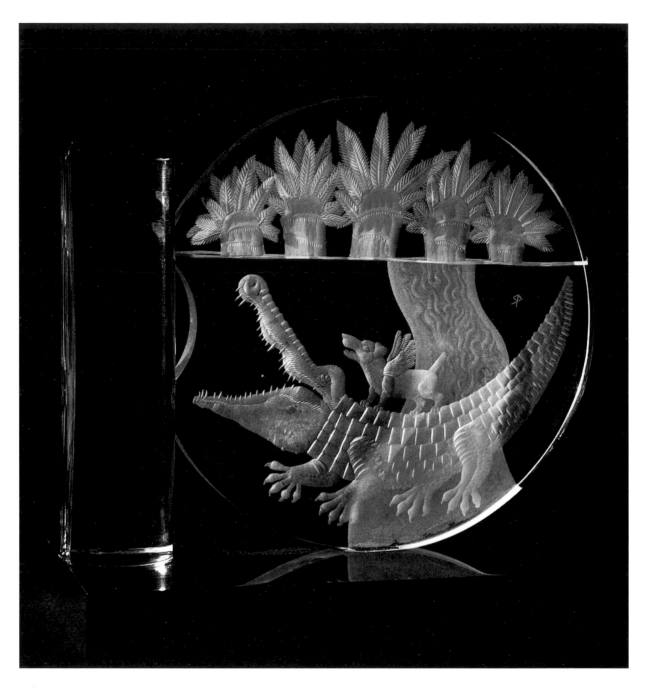

Between The Forest and The Water

Clear glass, wheel engraved with opaque base, 24 x 24 x 14cm, 1994.

A tribute to Monty (1976-1993), a fearless Jack Russell terrier who played a major role in the Pennell engravings, sharing many adventures. In real life he lived in a cottage between the woods and the River Wye. In this piece he is joined by his best adversary, the crocodile, in a more adventurous setting.

Wild Party

Bowl, clear glass, wheel engraved, 21 x 18cm, 1996.

This work shows a masked party in progress with the artist and his dog looking on as the dancers adopt wild postures. Metamorphosis made easy…

Natural Selection

The Mating Game

Bowl, over-cased rose tinted glass, wheel engraved, 20.5 x 16.5cm, 1996.

The boar is virile and eager, his mate calm and indifferent; he must be restrained while she is persuaded to comply. Analogous to human lust and love.

Natural Selection
Meeting
Bowl, brown over-cased glass, wheel engraved, 18 x 17cm, 1996.

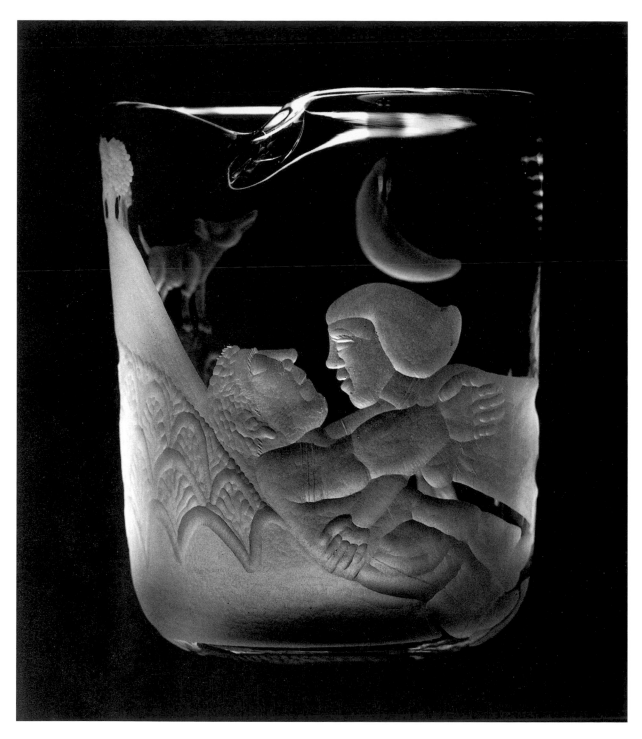

Lover's Moon
Bowl, clear glass, wheel engraved, 14 x 10.5cm, 1996.
Private Collection

Embracing in the moonlight, while a little dog stands guard over them.

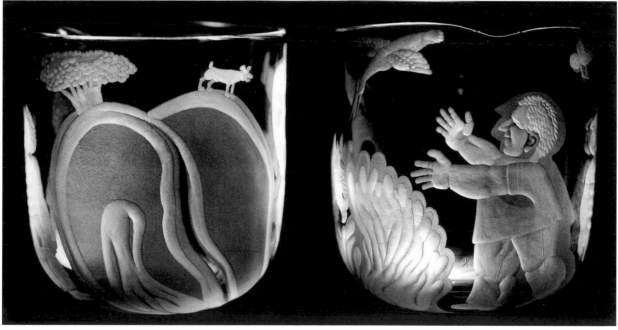

Falling and Diving

Bowl, green over-cased glass, 17 x 16cm, 1996.

Cox's Orange Pippin
Bronze relief, 29 x 28cm, 1997.

Cox's Orange Pippin

Intaglio print from an engraved glass plate, 26 x 18cm, 1997.

Getting The Bird
Bowl, clear glass, wheel engraved, 15.5 x 17cm, 1998.
Private Collection

Has several meanings in English. Is the bird in question flying? Or the woman sitting on the ground? Perhaps it is the harpy in a tree. It remains an enigma only the artist can solve.

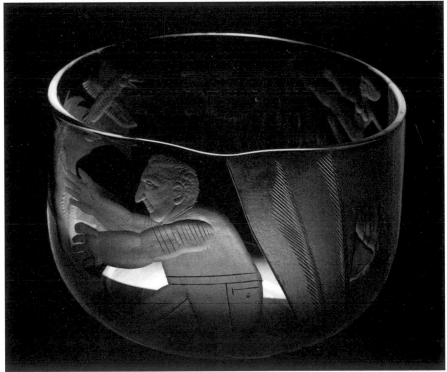

Tiger Burning
Bowl, clear glass, wheel engraved, 16 x 24cm, 1998.

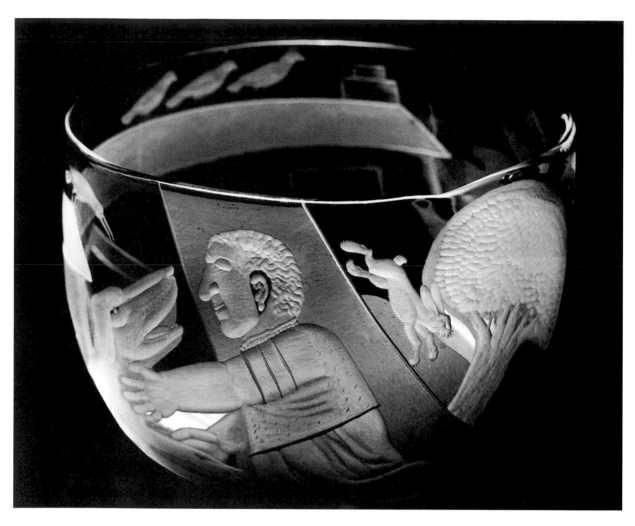

Welcome Home

Bowl, green over-cased glass, wheel engraved, 15 x 20cm, 1998.

Cycladic Mystery

Cut form bowl, 18 x 34cm, wheel engraved, 1999.

On this vessel the figures adopt the ritual posture of sculptures carved in the Cyclades for 2000 years, while modern man stands bemused.
Why was the right arm always folded under the left? Surely this is a great enigma, one of the great mysteries left to us by earlier cultures.

RONALD PENNELL

1952-56   Birmingham College of Art. Silversmithing, Design and Allied Crafts 1st Class Hons.

1956-57   Many awards including the Students Prize and a major German scholar–ship to study Glyptic

1959   Lecturer, Birmingham College of Art, elected ARBSA, FRSA

1964   Left teaching to establish freelance studio in Herefordshire with his wife, Betty Pennell

1964-74   Did not exhibit

1974-75   *Ronald Pennell Rock Crystal Engravings*, Crafts Council, London and British Tour

1977   Began to engrave glass

1979   Solo exhibition, *Ronald Pennell at Liberty's*, London

1979   Selected for Corning Museum *World Glass* Exhibition and World Tour

1979-80-81-85-93-95-97-99
    Selected for Corning Museum *New Glass Review*. One hundred works are selected from a world-wide entry

1982   Guest Lecturer, International Glass Symposium, Frauenau, Germany

1982   Guest Lecturer, International Glass Symposium, Baden/Vienna

1982   Guest Lecturer, 1st International Glass Symposium, Novy Bor, Czechoslovakia

1983   Awarded 2nd Prize, Fragile Art International Glass Competition, San Diego, USA

1988   Arts Channel Film, *Ronald Pennell Engraver*, for Welsh Arts Council

1988   Engraving Course Leader with Prof. Jiri Harcuba at Pilchuck Glass School, USA

1989   Awarded the Glass Sellers Prize, London with Amanda Brisbane

1990   Founder Member of BAFPA and Administrator of the Prize Fund

1992   Invited Artist, International Glass Engraving Symposium, Karlovy Vary, Czech Republic

1993   Elected to a Professorial Fellowship and awarded a Gold Medal, Academy of Arts, Architecture and Design, Prague

1990-92-95-98
    Selected for the Kanazawa International Glass Prize exhibitions, Japan

1993   One of ten invited foreign artists, *Glass '93* in Japan, JGAA

1994   Invited artist, *World Glass Now '94*, Hokkaido Museum of Modern Art

1995   Awarded Honorary Membership, Contemporary Applied Arts, London

1995   Awarded Finn Lynggaard Prize, *1st Kanazawa International Glass Triennale*, Japan

1996   Solo exhibition, Lobmeyr Gallery, Vienna

1996   Venezia Aperto Vetro, *1st International Glass Exhibition* at the Venice Biennale

1996   Guest lecturer, 1st International Glass Engraving Symposium, Kamenicky Senov. Awarded 'Highest Honour' by the Academy of Arts, Architecture and Design, Prague

1997	Invited artist, Hadelands Gallery, *A World of Glass* exhibition, Norway
1997	Guest lecturer, *Bildwerk*, Frauenau, Germany
1998	Visiting Professor of Glass Studies at the University of Wolverhampton, ongoing
1998	Awarded 'Honourable Mention', *2nd Kanazawa International Glass Triennale*, Japan
1998	Awarded Honorary Membership of the Dominik Bimann Society, Czech Republic
1999	Guest Professor, Institute of International Research in Glass, University of Sunderland
1999	The Shanghai Glass exhibition, University of Wolverhampton.
1999	Master Class at the Corning Studio, Corning Museum of Glass, New York State
1999	Awarded the Dominik Bimann International Gold Medal
1999-2001	Retrospective *Modern Myths The Art of Ronald Pennell* at Wolverhampton Art Gallery, Phillips International Auctioneers, London, The National Museum of Scotland, Edinburgh, National Glass Centre, Sunderland, Nottingham Castle Museum, Museum of Applied Arts, Prague

Work in Collections

British Museum, London, Ecology Medal
Corning Museum of Glass, New York State, USA
Crafts Council, London
Ebeltoft Museum, Denmark
French National Collection of Contemporary Art, Museum of Decorative Arts, Paris
Glass Museum, Dudley
Goldsmiths Hall, London
IGS Collection, Castle Lemberk, Czech Republic
Hereford Cathedral, 1300th Anniversary Medal
Hokkaido Museum of Modern Art, Japan
Museum of Glass, Kamenicky Senov, Czech Republic
HMS Manchester, given by Lady Cornford
Koganezaki Glass Museum, Japan
Moser Collection, Karlovy Vary, Czech Republic
Museum of Applied Arts, Prague
Norwich Castle Museum
Notojima Glass Museum, Japan
Nottingham Castle Museum
Pilchuck Collection at Pacific 1st Center, Seattle, USA
Portsmouth City Museum
Turner Museum, Sheffield University
Ulster Museum, Belfast, N. Ireland
Victoria & Albert Museum, London

BIBLIOGRAPHY

ARTICLES AND REVIEWS
DEUTSCHE GOLDSCHMIEDEZEITUNG 11/1968 'Glyptic von Ronald Pennell'
DEUTSCHE GRAVEURZEITUNG 1/1969 'Glyptic von Ronald Pennell'
CRAFTS 6/1974 'Ronald Pennell Gem Engraving'
THE CAMERA & THE CRAFTSMAN Crafts Council, London 1975
ANTIQUE COLLECTOR 6/1975 Gem Engraving Exhibition Review
DEUTSCHE GOLDSCHMIEDEZEITUNG 6/1977 'Pennell Gems and Medals'
CRAFTS 28/1975 Masterpiece Exhibition Review
Celia Hall HOMES & GARDENS September 1979 'Crystal Clear Wit' Engravings
by Ronald Pennell
LIFE Magazine 4/1979 'Art in Glass'
NEW GLASS 1979 The Corning Museum of Glass NY. A World Survey
AMERICAN CRAFT Oct/Nov 1980
CREFFT 21/1981 Welsh Arts Council
Peta Levi HOUSE & GARDEN 8/1981 'British Glass'
Dillon Clarke NEUES GLAS Düsseldorf 4/1981 'British Glass'
NEW GLASS REVIEW 2. 1981 The Corning Museum of Glass NY. A World
Survey
NEW GLASS REVIEW 3. 1982 The Corning Museum of Glass NY. A World Survey
CRAFT QUARTERLY 1/Spring 1982 Northern Arts 'Ronald Pennell Portfolio'
CRAFT QUARTERLY 4/Summer 1982 Northern Arts 'Ronald Pennell Glass
Engraving'
Megan Tressider INTERIORS 1/1982 'Glass of '82'
NEUES GLAS 1/1983 exhibition review
CZECH ARTS & CRAFTS Prague 1/1983 'International Glass Symposium'
Jiri Harcuba CZECH ARTS & CRAFTS Prague 2/1983 'Ryt-Sklo Ronald Pennell'
Dr Mathilde Grunewald NEUES GLAS Düsseldorf 3/1984 'Outlook on Life –
Ronald Pennell'
CZECH GLASS REVIEW Prague 3/1983 'IGS Symposium Novy Bor'
PRESENT Magazine Coburg 8/1985 '2nd Coburg Prize review'
Jane Norrie ARTS REVIEW Aug/1985 'Betty and Ronald Pennell'
NEW GLASS REVIEW 7. 1986 The Corning Museum of Glass NY. A World
Survey
CONTEMPORARY BRITISH MEDALS British Museum 1986
Jane Norrie ARTS REVIEW 1988 'The Refinement of the Species' Oxford
Gallery review
Jane Freeman CRAFTS 11/1991 'Human Interest' at Gainsborough's House,
Sudbury
CREFFT 60/1991 'International Recognition for Ronald Pennell'
CREFFT 63/1992 1st International Glass Engraving Symposium, Karlovy Vary,
Czech Republic
Eva Schmitt NEUES GLAS 4/1992 Exhibition review
THE MEDAL Spring 1992 'BAMS The First Ten Years'
IN THE ROUND – Contemporary Art Medals of the World, British Museum
THE MEDAL 1993
NEW GLASS REVIEW 14.1993 The Corning Museum of Glass NY. A World
Survey

D'Este Bond CRAFTS Jan/Feb 1994 'Taking Sides'
THE MEDAL 24 Spring 1994 British Art Medal Society
THE MEDAL 26 Spring 1995 British Art Medal Society
Antoinette Fay-Halle MASTERPIECES OF CONTEMPORARY GLASS National Museum of Ceramics, Sèvres 1995
NEW GLASS REVIEW 16 1995 The Corning Museum of Glass NY. A World Survey
NEW GLASS REVIEW 18 1996 The Corning Museum of Glass NY. A World Survey
NEW GLASS REVIEW 19 1999 The Corning Museum of Glass NY. A World Survey

BOOKS
The SATURDAY BOOK 33. 'Gem Engravings by Ronald Pennell'
Joan Bamford 'ANTIQUE COLLECTING FOR THE FUTURE' London 1976
Maria Schofield DECORATIVE ART & MODERN INTERIORS Studio Vista London 1978
Maria Schofield DECORATIVE ART & MODERN INTERIORS Studio Vista London 1979
Alban Donez GLASS-Animals, Abrams New York 1986
Dan Klein 'GLASS – A Contemporary Art' Rizzoli New York 1988
Susan K. Frantz 'CONTEMPORARY GLASS' – A World Wide Survey from the Corning Museum 1989
Tsuneo Yoshimizu 'THE SURVEY OF GLASS IN THE WORLD' Kyuryodo Art Publishers, Japan 1992
Peter Layton 'GLASS ART' A & C Black London 1996
Edited by Attilia Dorigato & Dan Klein 'INTERNATIONAL NEW GLASS' Arsenale Editrice, Italy 1996
Edited by Atsushi Takeda 'KOGANEZAKI GLASS MUSEUM – Contemporary Glass Collection' 1997
Marilyn and Tom Goodearl 'GLASS ENGRAVING – International Contemporary Artists' Antique Collectors' Club 1999
Atsushi Takeda 'EXPRESSION – Contemporary Glass' Yurindo Co. Ltd. Publishers, Japan

FILM
Welsh Arts 'Ronald Pennell – Engraver' ARTS CHANNEL FILM for television 1988

EXHIBITIONS (from 1974 only)

1974	London Crafts Council Gallery and British Tour, 'Ronald Pennell Rock Crystal Engraving' *Folder ill*
1975	London Cameo Corner (*solo*)
1975	London Crafts Council Gallery and Tour, 'Everyman a Patron'
1975	Cardiff National Museum of Wales, 'Three Artists'
1975	London Crafts Council Gallery, 'The Camera and the Craftsman' *catalogue*
1976	London The Design Centre, 'British Crafts'
1976	London Goldsmiths' Hall, 'Loot'
1977	London Victoria & Albert Museum, 'Man Made'
1977	London British Crafts Centre 'Masterpiece' *catalogue*
1977	Birmingham Polytechnic (*solo*)
1977	Wolverhampton Polytechnic, 'Betty and Ronald Pennell'
1977	East Midlands Arts Touring Exhibition *catalogue*
1978	Birmingham West Midlands Arts Centre + Tour, 'Craftsmen at Home' *photographed by Cliff Guttridge*
1978	Oslo, Norway, 'British Craftsmen at the Galleri Marjatta'
1979	Portsmouth City Museum and Art Gallery, 'Glass Now', *catalogue*
1979	Corning NY USA Corning Museum of Glass, 'New Glass – A World Wide Survey' *catalogue*
1979	London 'Ronald Pennell at Liberty's'
1979	London British Crafts Centre, Crafts for the Child
1979	Erbach, Germany, German Ivory Museum, 'Ivory and Gold' International Design Exhibition
1979	Portsmouth City Museum and Art Gallery, Glass Decorators Exhibition *catalogue*
1979	London Mall Galleries IYC exhibition by Spink Modern Collections
1980	Edinburgh Scottish Crafts Centre, 'Craftwork Heals'
1980	Hereford, Hereford City Museum and Art Gallery, *Invited Artist*
1980	Birmingham, City Museum and Art Gallery, 'Showcase' (*solo*)
1980	Sotheby's 'Contemporary British Crafts' *catalogue*
1980	Michigan USA Habatat Galleries, 'Ten Concepts' *catalogue*
1980	Boston USA Westminster Gallery, 'British Crafts'
1980	Edinburgh Scottish Crafts Centre , 'British Artists in Glass'
1980	London Heals, 'Goblets from the British Artists in Glass'
1981	London Victoria & Albert Museum, 'New Glass' *catalogue*
1981	London British Crafts Centre, 'BAG'
1981	Sheffield, Mappin Art Gallery, 'BAG'
1981	Sunderland Museum and Art Gallery, 'BAG'
1981	Lucerne, Switzerland, Glas-Galerie 'Engraved Glass'
1981	Michigan, USA Habatat Galleries, *Gallery artist*
1981	Cardiff, Welsh Arts Council Tour
1982	London, Dan Klein Gallery
1982	Lucerne, Switzerland, Glas-Galerie, Glaskunst aus Grossbritannien *catalogue*
1982	Frankfurt, Germany, La Galleria, Glaskunst aus Grossbritannien *catalogue*

1982	Bremen, Germany, Monica Trujen Gallery, 'Zauber einer Kugel' *catalogue*
1982	Novy Bor, Czechoslovakia, IGS. 1st International Glass Symposium *catalogue*
1982	Prague, Czechoslovakia, Museum of Applied Arts, 'IGS exhibition'
1982	Frauenau, Germany, Glass Museum, IGS, 'Glas unserer Zeit in Kunst und Handwerk' *catalogue*
1982	Worms, Germany, Museum der Stadt Worms 'Modernes Glas'
1982	Oxford, The Oxford Gallery *(solo)*
1983	San Diego, USA, Fine Arts Gallery, Fragile Art *2nd Prize Winner*
1983	Austin, Texas, USA, Matrix Gallery *(solo)*
1983	Lexington MA, USA, Gallery on the Green *(solo)*
1983	Liverpool Bluecoat Gallery 'Prescote Group exhibition'
1983	Cardiff, Wales, St. Davids Hall *(solo)*
1983	Munich, Germany, Glas-Galerie Nordend 'Glaskunst aus Gross britannien' *catalogue*
1983	Sunderland Arts Centre and Tour, 'British Studio Glass' *catalogue*
1984	Amsterdam, Netherlands, De Rozengalerie 'Harcuba, Pennell and Touskova' *catalogue*
1984	London, Dan Klein Gallery 'Jiri Harcuba and Ronald Pennell'
1984	London, Coleridge of Piccadilly 'Opening exhibition'
1984	Aldeburgh, Aldeburgh Festival Gallery 'Jiri Harcuba and Ronald Pennell'
1984	Michigan, USA, Habatat Galleries, 'Harcuba-Pennell-Kohler' *Folder ill*
1984	Veltheim, Germany, Glas-Galerie Veltheim 'Glaskunst aus Gross britannien
1985	Kingswinford, Broadfield House Glass Museum 'Jiri Harcuba and Ronald Pennell'
1985	London, British Crafts Centre 'British Studio Glass'
1985	Coburg, Germany, Schloss Coburg '2nd Coburg Glass Prize Exhibition' *catalogue*
1985	Stockholm, Sweden 'XX FIDEM Congress Exhibition of Medallic Art' *catalogue*
1986	Hamburg, Germany, Galerie L
1986	Florida, USA, Loch Haven Art Center 'European Studio Glass' *catalogue*
1986	London, Coleridge Glass *(solo)*
1987	Bremen, Germany, Monica Trujen Gallery 'Glas'
1987	Hamburg, Germany, Galerie L
1987	Munich, Germany, First Glass Gallery
1987	Michigan and Florida, USA, Habatat Galleries *Gallery Artists*
1997	Corning NY, USA, Corning Museum of Glass 'Thirty Years of New Glass' *catalogue*
1997	Ohio, USA, Toledo Museum of Art 'Thirty Years of New Glass'
1988	Bremen, Germany, Monica Trujen Gallery 'Glas'
1988	Kuala Lumpur, Malaysia, 'British Glass' *catalogue*
1988	London, 'Sotheby's Decorative Art Prize Exhibition' *catalogue*
1988	Oxford, The Oxford Gallery *(solo)*
1988	Seattle, USA, Pilchuck Glass School Faculty Exhibition
1989	Tokyo, Japan, Nakama Gallery

1989	Bremen, Germany, Monica Trujen Gallery 'Glas'
1989	Michigan, USA, Habatat Galleries 'Scale Detail' *catalogue*
1990	Tokyo, Japan, Nakama Gallery 'World Glass Selection'
1990	Japan, 'Kanazawa International Prize Exhibition' *catalogue*
1990	Washington State, USA, The Sheehan Gallery at Whitman College 'British Crafts' *catalogue*
1990	Washington State University Museum of Art
1990	London, Opus 1 Gallery 'British Glass'
1990	Llangollen, Wales, at the European Centre for Traditional and Regional Cultures
1991	followed by a British Tour 'The Ulster Museum European Glass Collection'
1991	London, Christie's Decorative Art *catalogue*
1991	Sudbury, Gainsborough's House 'Human Interest'
1991	Tokyo, Japan, Gallery Nakama '100 Goblets'
1991	Clyro, Kilvert Gallery 'Ronald Pennell' *Carved and Painted Wood Sculptures* 'Betty Pennell' *Paintings*
1992	London, Bonhams 'Decorative Art Today' *catalogue*
1992	Cologne, Germany, Kunsthaus am Museum *Group exhibition Invited artist*
1992	London, Christie's Decorative Art *catalogue*
1992	Tokyo, Japan, Gallery Nakama *Group exhibition*
1992	Karlovy Vary, Czechoslovakia '1st International Glass Engraving Symposium' *Invited Artist, catalogue*
1992	Japan, 'Kanazawa International Glass Prize exhibition' *catalogue*
1992	London, The British Museum '23rd FIDEM Congress Exhibition' *catalogue*
1993	London, Crafts Council Gallery and British Tour 'The Glass Show' *catalogue*
1993	Oxford, The Oxford Gallery, 25th Anniversary Exhibition, *Invited artist*
1993	London, Crafts Council Gallery 'A Vision of Craft'
1993	London, Christie's Decorative Art *catalogue*
1993	Tokyo, Japan, Japan Glass Art Association, Japan Glass '93 *Invited Foreign Artist, catalogue*
1993	Tokyo, Japan, Odakyu Museum, Japan Glass '93
1993	Osaka, Japan, Daimaru Museum, Japan Glass '93
1993	Fukuoka, Japan, Iwataya Exhibition Hall, Japan Glass '93
1993	Edinburgh, Scotland,The Scottish Gallery *Group exhibition*
1994	Farnham, New Ashgate Gallery, 3-person show 'Engravers Images'
1994	Bavaria, Germany, Schloss Theuern 'European Engraved Glass' *catalogue*
1994	Hokkaido, Japan, Hokkaido Museum of Modern Art, World Glass '94 *Invited artist, catalogue*
1994	Newent, The Glassbarn *Group exhibition*
1995	Hove, Museum and Art Gallery *Group exhibition, Invited Artist*
1995	Japan, '1st Kanazawa International Glass Triennale' Awarded Finn Lynggaard Prize *catalogue*
1995	Birmingham, MAC, Craftspace Touring Exhibition 'Made in the Middle' *Invited artist, catalogue*
1995	Sèvres, France, National Museum of Ceramics 'Masterpieces of Contemporary Glass' *catalogue*

1995	Newent, Cowdy Gallery *Group exhibition*
1996	Hereford, Museum and Art Gallery *Invited Group exhibition*
1996	Vienna, Austria, Lobmeyr Gallery *(solo)*
1996	Venice, Italy, Venice Biennale 'Venezia Aperto Vetro' *catalogue*
1996	Kamenicky Senov, Czech Republic 'International Glass Engraving Symposium' *catalogue*
1996	Kamenicky Senov, Czech Republic, Glass Museum
1996	Novy-Bor, Czech Republic, Galerie Wunsch
1996	Newent, Cowdy Gallery
1996	London, The Glass Art Gallery 'British Studio Glass'
1997	St. Helens, Pilkington Glass Museum, 90's Glass
1997	Wrexham, Middlesbrough and Bexley 'New Glass in Context' + Crafts Council Collection *(selection)*
1997	Cardiff, Wales, Crafts in the Bay, 90's Glass
1997	Oslo, Norway, Hadelands Gallery, 'World Glass' *Invited artist catalogue*
1998	London, Contemporary Applied Arts – Ronald Pennell in Focus
1998	Denmark, International Glass – Ebeltoft Museum
1998	Japan, Kanazawa International Triennale *(Awarded Honourable Mention)*
1998	Sunderland,Glass UK, National Glass Centre
1999	Shanghai, China, New Glass Economy Contemporary British Glass from the University of Wolverhampton *catalogue*